Framework Overview

The *English Language Arts/English Language Development Framework for California Public Schools: Kindergarten Through Grade Twelve* (*ELA/ELD Framework*) offers guidance for providing all California students a world-class education in English language arts and in literacy in history/ social studies, science, and technical subjects. In addition, it offers guidance for supporting English learners' progress in English language development. The state's more than six and one quarter million public-school students in transitional kindergarten through grade twelve come from a range of ethnic backgrounds; speak a variety of home languages or dialects of English; live in different social and economic circumstances; are being raised in different geographic, community, and familial settings; have different cultural experiences and histories; and have different physical and cognitive abilities. Many are learning English as an additional language.

The *ELA/ELD Framework* breaks new ground by providing a blueprint for the implementation of two sets of interrelated standards: the California Common Core State Standards for English Language Arts and Literacy in History/Social Studies, Science, and Technical Subjects (CA CCSS for ELA/Literacy) and the California English Language Development Standards (CA ELD Standards). These two sets of standards have wide-ranging importance. The ability to read, write, and communicate with competence and confidence in English across a range of personal and academic contexts expands students' opportunities for career and college success, full and wise participation in a democratic society and global economy, and achievement of their personal aspirations.

Moreover, skill in literacy and language provides individuals with access to extraordinary and powerful literature that widens perspectives, illuminates the human experience, and deepens understandings of self and others. And, because literacy and language are foundational to all learning, both sets of standards play a crucial role in ensuring that California students achieve content standards in every subject area. Therefore, the *ELA/ELD Framework* is a valuable resource for educators of every discipline.

The following guiding principles and beliefs informed the development of the framework. (See the introduction to the framework for discussions.)

- Schooling should help all students achieve their highest potential.
- The responsibility for learners' literacy and language development is shared.
- ELA/literacy and ELD curricula should be well designed, comprehensive, and integrated.
- Effective teaching is essential to student success.
- Motivation and engagement play crucial roles in learning.

This executive summary provides highlights from the framework and directs readers to resources in the document. It begins with a broad overview of the standards and California's vision for their implementation, features important grade-level guidance, and highlights selected topics crucial for effective implementation.

Distinctive Features of the *ELA/ELD Framework*

The ELA/ELD Framework

▶ provides guidance for implementation of two sets of standards: CA CCSS for ELA/Literacy and CA ELD Standards;

▶ promotes an integrated and interdisciplinary approach to literacy and language instruction;

▶ discusses literacy and language instruction in terms of five crosscutting themes: Meaning Making, Language Development, Effective Expression, Content Knowledge, and Foundational Skills;

▶ advocates for a range of reading in school and through organized independent reading;

▶ positions cultural diversity, multilingualism, and biliteracy as valuable resources and assets;

▶ applies to all content areas;

▶ presents numerous examples of a comprehensive approach to ELD, which includes both integrated and designated ELD;

▶ reflects research and includes brief snapshots and lengthier vignettes of practice;

▶ provides guidance for teaching the range of California's learners, highlighting issues of access and equity;

▶ integrates 21st century learning throughout ELA/literacy and ELD instruction;

▶ emphasizes the shared responsibility for literacy and language instruction among educators;

▶ calls for collaboration among students, educators (including classroom teachers, specialists, and school and district administrators), families, and communities.

The Standards

Students who achieve the **CA CCSS for ELA/Literacy** develop the skills in reading, writing, speaking, and listening that are the foundation for any creative and purposeful expression in language. They are able to undertake the close, attentive reading that is at the heart of understanding and enjoying complex works of literature. Students exhibit the capacities of a literate individual: They demonstrate independence; they build strong content knowledge; they respond to the varying demands of audience, task, purpose, and discipline; they comprehend as well as critique; they value evidence; they use technology and digital media strategically and capably; and they come to understand other perspectives and cultures.

As described in chapter 1 of the *ELA/ELD Framework*, the CA CCSS for ELA/Literacy emphasize the development of these broad capacities and highlight, in particular, the importance of content-rich informational texts; responding and arguing from textual evidence; and complex texts and academic language. The College and Career Readiness Anchor Standards broadly describe the skills and understandings that students should demonstrate in each of four strands—Reading, Writing, Speaking and Listening, and Language—as they enter postsecondary education and the workforce. Additional specificity is provided by grade-level (K–8) and grade-span (9–10 and 11–12) standards. The domains of literature, informational text, and, in kindergarten through grade five, foundational skills are addressed in Reading. Separate Literacy Standards in History/Social Studies, Science, and Technical Subjects are provided for grades six through twelve.

The **CA ELD Standards** are aligned to the CA CCSS for ELA/Literacy as they amplify (magnify and make clear) areas of English language development that are crucial for academic learning. The standards emphasize language learning as a social process and language itself as a complex and dynamic meaning-making resource. They promote the notion of supporting English learner (EL) students to develop awareness that different languages and variations of English exist and that their home languages and cultures are valuable resources in their own right and useful for building proficiency in English.

The standards help teachers support EL students to interact in meaningful ways with others and with complex texts, engage in and learn through intellectually challenging tasks across the content areas, develop academic English, and develop awareness about how English works so that they can use it intentionally and purposefully. The standards also provide guidance on teaching foundational skills to English learners, taking into account a variety of factors, including literacy proficiency in the primary language.

The CA ELD Standards are stated by grade level (K–8) and grade spans (9–10 and 11–12) according to the English Language Development Proficiency Level Continuum, which distinguishes three overall English language development levels: Emerging, Expanding, and Bridging. Importantly, the standards position ELs at all English language proficiency levels as capable of high-level thinking and meaningful engagement with complex, cognitively demanding academic tasks in English as long as they are provided appropriate types and levels of scaffolding.

General Progression in the CA ELD Standards ELD Continuum

ELD Continuum				
Native Language	⟶ Emerging ⟶	Expanding ⟶	Bridging ⟶	Lifelong Language Learners

The Big Picture of California's ELA/Literacy and ELD Instruction

The Circles of Implementation graphic (presented below and described here and in chapter 2 of the *ELA/ELD Framework*) provides the big picture of implementation of ELA/literacy and ELD instruction. The outer ring displays the overarching goals. By the time California's students complete high school they have

- developed the readiness for college, careers, and civic life;
- attained the capacities of literate individuals;
- become broadly literate;
- acquired the skills for living and learning in the 21st century.

The white field in the graphic represents the context in which instruction occurs. The *ELA/ELD Framework* calls for an instructional context that is integrated, motivating, engaging, respectful, and intellectually challenging for all students at all grade levels.

Circling the standards are the key crosscutting themes of the standards. Instruction across the strands of ELA/literacy (Reading, Writing, Speaking and Listening, and Language) and the parts of ELD (Interacting in Meaningful Ways, Learning About How English Works, and Using Foundational Skills) focuses on **Meaning Making, Language Development, Effective Expression, Content Knowledge,** and **Foundational Skills**. These themes highlight the interconnections among the strands of the CA CCSS for ELA/Literacy and the parts of the CA ELD Standards.

In the center of the graphic are the two sets of standards, which define grade-level year-end expectations for student knowledge and abilities and guide instructional planning. The standards are the pathway to achieving the overarching goals of ELA/literacy and ELD instruction.

Key Themes of ELA/Literacy and ELD Instruction

Instruction focuses on...

Meaning Making

Meaning making is at the heart of ELA/literacy and ELD instruction. It is the central purpose for interacting with text, producing text, engaging in research, participating in discussion, and giving presentations. It is the reason for learning the foundational skills and for expanding language. Meaning making includes literal understanding but is not confined to it at any grade or with any student. Inference making and critical reading, writing, and listening are given substantial and explicit attention in every discipline. Among the contributors to meaning making are language, knowledge, motivation, and in the case of reading and writing, the ability to recognize printed words and use the alphabetic code to express ideas.

Language Development

Language is the cornerstone of literacy and learning. It is with and through language that students learn, think, and express information, ideas, perspectives, and questions. The strands of the CA CCSS for ELA/Literacy—Reading, Writing, Speaking and Listening, and Language—all have language at the core, as do the parts of the CA ELD Standards—Interacting in Meaningful Ways, Learning About How English Works, and Using Foundational Literacy Skills. Students enrich their language as they read, write, speak, and listen and as they interact with one another and learn about language. The foundational skills provide access to written language.

Effective Expression

Each strand of the CA CCSS for ELA/Literacy and each part of the CA ELD Standards includes attention to effective expression. Students learn to examine the author's craft as they read, analyzing how authors use language, text structure, and images to convey information, influence their readers, and evoke responses. Students learn to effectively express themselves as writers, discussion partners, and presenters, and they use digital media and visual displays to enhance their expression. They gain command over the conventions of written and spoken English, and they learn to communicate in ways appropriate for the context and task.

Content Knowledge

Content knowledge is a powerful contributor to comprehension of text. It also undergirds the ability to write effective opinions/arguments, narratives, and explanatory/informational text; engage in meaningful discussions; and present ideas and information to others. It contributes significantly to language development, and it is fundamental to learning about how English works. Both sets of standards ensure that students can learn from informational texts and can share their knowledge as writers and speakers. An organized independent reading program contributes to knowledge. Content knowledge has a powerful reciprocal relationship with the development of literacy and language.

Foundational Skills

Acquisition of the foundational skills enables students to independently read and use written language to learn about the world and themselves; experience extraordinary and diverse works of literary fiction and nonfiction; and share their knowledge, ideas, stories, and perspectives with others. Students who know how to decode and develop automaticity with an increasing number of words are best positioned to make significant strides in meaning making, language development, effective expression, and content knowledge. At the same time, attention to those themes provides the very reason for learning about the alphabetic code and propels progress in the foundational skills. (See the Resource Guide to the Foundational Skills at www.cde.ca.gov/ci/rl/cf/documents/foundskillswhitepaper.pdf.)

English Language Development Instruction

California's EL students should be provided comprehensive ELD, which includes both *integrated* and *designated* ELD instruction. English learners enter school at different ages and with a range of cultural and linguistic backgrounds, socioeconomic conditions, experiences with formal schooling, proficiencies in their primary language(s) and in English, as well as other experiences in the home, school, and community. Many were born in the U.S., and others come from nations all over the world. In short, they are a heterogeneous group of individuals. All of California's ELs are learning English as an additional language while simultaneously engaging in intellectually challenging and content-rich instruction. It is incumbent upon every educator to understand California's model of comprehensive ELD instruction.

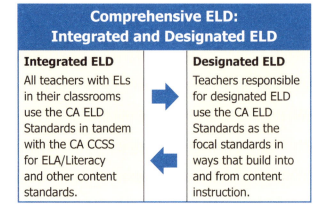

Integrated ELD instruction occurs throughout the school day in every subject area by every teacher who has an EL student in the classroom. The CA ELD Standards are used in tandem with the CA CCSS for ELA/Literacy and other content standards to ensure students strengthen their abilities to use academic English as they learn content through English.

Comprehensive ELD: Integrated and Designated ELD

Integrated ELD	Designated ELD
All teachers with ELs in their classrooms use the CA ELD Standards in tandem with the CA CCSS for ELA/Literacy and other content standards.	Teachers responsible for designated ELD use the CA ELD Standards as the focal standards in ways that build into and from content instruction.

Designated ELD is provided to ELs during a protected time in the regular school day. Teachers use the CA ELD Standards as the focal standards in ways that build into and from content instruction to develop critical language ELs need for content learning in English. Ideally, students are grouped for designated ELD by English language proficiency levels (Emerging, Expanding, Bridging), although schools need to consider their particular student population (e.g., number of ELs at each proficiency level) and make appropriate decisions about grouping.

English language development instruction ensures that ELs use English purposefully; interact in meaningful ways with peers, content, and texts; and learn about how English works, as illustrated in the figure below.

In the framework, pairs of vignettes in each grade level (for transitional kindergarten through grade 8) and grade span (grades 9–10 and 11–12) illustrate (1) integrated ELD instruction in the context of a content area and (2) designated ELD instruction that builds into and from the content. Many shorter snapshots of practice in the framework describe effective practices in ELD instruction.

Grade-Level Guidance

The grade-level chapters in the *ELA/ELD Framework* are organized into grade spans. Elementary school content and pedagogy are addressed in chapters 3–5, which cover transitional kindergarten through grade one, grades two and three, and grades four and five, respectively. Chapter 6 provides guidance for middle school—grades six, seven, and eight. Chapter 7 focuses on high school, with attention to grades nine and ten and grades eleven and twelve. Each chapter includes the following features as they pertain to the specific grade levels:

- Discussions of content and pedagogy for each grade level (or grade span in the case of grades nine and ten and eleven and twelve) organized in terms of the key themes (Meaning Making, Language Development, Effective Expression, Content Knowledge, and Foundational Skills)

- Descriptions of and suggestions for integrated and designated ELD instruction

- At least ten snapshots of practice, including integrated English language arts, literacy in the content areas, integrated ELD, and designated ELD

- Two lengthy vignettes of practice for each grade level (or, in the case of high school, grade span), one that illustrates ELA or literacy in a content area along with integrated ELD and the other that provides a detailed example of designated ELD that builds from and into the content of the first vignette

- Numerous figures that provide information on crucial areas of ELA/literacy or ELD content or pedagogy (e.g., developmentally appropriate environments and practices for young children [chapter 3], descriptions of stages of spelling development [chapter 4], discussant roles in literature circles [chapter 5], elements of effective adolescent writing instruction [chapter 6], ways to prepare an effective Socratic seminar [chapter 7])

- Samples of student writing with annotations

- A section titled "Supporting Students Strategically" that delineates research findings on effective teaching practices with students experiencing difficulty with literacy

In addition, each chapter reinforces the importance of careful planning that anticipates year-end and unit goals, responds to students' needs (as determined by skillful formative assessment), and incorporates the framing questions from the *ELA/ELD Framework* displayed in the figure below.

Every grade is a crucial part of the continuum of learning toward students' achievement of the overarching goals of ELA/literacy and ELD instruction. Because California's students are diverse in terms of their progress along the continuum, teachers should be familiar with the content and practices of preceding and subsequent grades.

Framing Questions for All Students	Add for English Learners
▸ What are the big ideas and culminating performance tasks of the larger unit of study, and how does this lesson build toward them?	▸ What are the English language proficiency levels of my students?
▸ What are the learning targets for this lesson, and what should students be able to do at the end of the lesson?	▸ Which CA ELD Standards amplify the CA CCSS for ELA/Literacy at students' English language proficiency levels?
▸ Which clusters of CA CCSS for ELA/Literacy does this lesson address?	▸ What language might be new for students and/or present challenges?
▸ What background knowledge, skills, and experiences do my students have related to this lesson?	▸ How will students interact in meaningful ways and learn about how English works in collaborative, interpretive, and/or productive modes?
▸ How complex are the texts and tasks that I will use?	
▸ How will students make meaning, express themselves effectively, develop language, and learn content? How will they apply or learn foundational skills?	
▸ What types of scaffolding, accommodations, or modifications will individual students need to effectively engage in the lesson tasks?	
▸ How will my students and I monitor learning during and after the lesson, and how will that inform instruction?	

Transitional Kindergarten Through Grade One

The first years of schooling are a profoundly important time on the pathway to literacy, and the quality of the curricula and instruction offered to children in the transitional kindergarten through grade one span has long-lasting implications.

During these crucial years, children acquire the skills, knowledge, and dispositions that establish the foundation for a lifetime of learning. Instruction is carefully specified and strategically sequenced, and rich, authentic experiences are provided in a developmentally appropriate environment. Instruction recognizes and responds to children's social-emotional, physical, and cognitive needs, all of which are critical to long-term literacy development. Young learners move and explore, engage in hands-on investigations, and interact freely and in structured ways with a range of peers and adults on interesting topics. They participate in self-directed and teacher-directed learning experiences.

Content and pedagogy in the grade span include the following:

- **Meaning Making** – Children engage meaningfully with others and with a range of texts as listeners, writers, and readers. They learn to ask and answer questions to clarify and convey meaning. They are introduced to comprehension strategies and a variety of text structures, and they participate in conversations to share understandings about texts and topics. Teachers select texts purposefully to support comprehension development, and they establish an engaging and motivating context in which to teach and foster reading comprehension.

- **Language Development** – Because language is acquired largely through *exposure to* and *purposeful use of* language in a range of meaningful contexts, teachers establish language-rich environments. They model broad vocabulary and varied grammatical and discourse structures as they interact with children, deliver instruction, facilitate learning experiences across the curricula, and discuss classroom routines. They read aloud texts that stretch children's language, engage children in genuine discussions about a range of topics using academic language, and provide stimulating social learning activities and investigations that fuel conversations.

- **Effective Expression** – Children express themselves in writing by dictating their ideas to adults and by using pictures, marks, and their emerging knowledge of the alphabetic system. They learn how to participate in discussions (taking turns and listening attentively) and how to express their ideas more formally, such as through "show and tell" and other presentations. Their knowledge of language conventions expands through rich exposure and reflections on language.

- **Content Knowledge** – Children engage in many hands-on explorations, participate in shared research projects and rich content instruction, and interact with informational text as listeners and beginning readers. Although there are many opportunities to pursue topics of personal interest, teachers also ensure that knowledge is built systematically by providing text sets (several books on a topic under investigation) so that concepts and domain-specific language are repeated and built upon.

- **Foundational Skills** – Children manipulate and reflect on the sounds of spoken language as they sing, engage with books that draw attention to the sounds of words, and play language games. They increase their familiarity with the alphabetic system, learning letter-sound and spelling-sound correspondences. They apply their knowledge as they read simple text consisting of regular patterns and as they write for their own purposes. They learn relevant sight words in meaningful contexts.

> **Among many figures included in chapter 3 are ones that**
>
> ▸ share research on motivation and engagement;
>
> ▸ describe appropriate literacy and language environments and practices for young children;
>
> ▸ suggest ways to provide young children access to informational text;
>
> ▸ define phonics and word recognition terminology;
>
> ▸ describe the importance of developing children's independence with the alphabetic code.

English learners engage with the same intellectually stimulating content through careful scaffolding and guidance provided by the CA ELD Standards. At the same time, they are learning English as an additional language and are receiving instruction that attends to their steady progress along the ELD continuum. The cultural and language resources young children bring to the classroom are capitalized on in integrated and designated ELD instruction. Special attention is given to oral language development during this grade span. Learning about language occurs in meaningful, relevant contexts. Daily engagement with a range of language and literacy tasks is critical for English language development (including singing, being read to, exploring books with peers, engaging in conversations, retelling stories and events, and many other learning tasks).

Transitional Kindergarten

Transitional kindergarten programs capitalize on young children's active, social, and inquisitive natures. Teachers draw on the California Preschool Learning Foundations to support children's progress toward the Kindergarten CA CCSS for ELA/Literacy and, as appropriate, the CA ELD Standards. Language development is a crucial focus of the ELA/literacy curriculum this year, and children learn to listen attentively to their peers and adults as well as to express their own thoughts. They use language purposefully, and they notice language as they make language choices and witness the impact of their words and as they play with speech sounds.

Children have many opportunities to interact with print in meaningful contexts—print that answers their questions (e.g., books), serves a purpose (e.g., labels on cubbies), and is a written record of their ideas (e.g., a caption for a painting dictated to an adult). Importantly, learning about print is not simply learning to recite the alphabet and copy letters. Learning about print entails discovering the personal value of print and the conventions of printed language. Teachers create print-rich environments, and children find print—and the tools to generate their own printed messages—in learning centers throughout the setting. Transitional kindergarteners have coherent experiences with content (e.g., science, social studies) appropriate for their age, backgrounds, and interests and that build toward kindergarten content standards.

Among the guidance and instructional suggestions for transitional kindergarten programs are ways to support children's progress in discussion (pp. 175–176), sentence starters to prompt small group or partner discussions (p. 176), tips for ensuring young children's access to informational text (pp. 178–179), suggestions for fostering phonological awareness (pp. 182–183), and research-based practices for supporting language development of young children who may have language delays (p. 174).

Kindergarten

Kindergarteners learn through play, social interactions, and teacher-directed instruction. Children increase their understanding of the purposes of print as they engage daily with a wide variety of texts and in their own daily attempts to express their ideas and knowledge in writing. Instruction includes a significant focus on how print works, and kindergarten children make considerable progress in understanding the logic of the alphabetic code, especially letter-sound relationships and initial decoding of simple, regular words.

Reading aloud daily from high-quality texts is a high priority for teachers in that it serves to broaden children's language and their knowledge of the natural and social world, while also stirring their imaginations and igniting their curiosity. Teachers engage in thinking aloud about texts to model comprehension strategies, and children talk a great deal with one another about texts and other learning experiences.

The chief differences between **transitional kindergarten** and **kindergarten** programs are the pacing, expectations, and amount of learning situated in play. Transitional kindergarteners move more slowly through the curricula, making progress toward achievement of the kindergarten CA CCSS for ELA/Literacy without the expectation of mastery, and they have more opportunities to engage in literacy and language activities in playful contexts. Importantly, *throughout the transitional kindergarten through grade one span* children learn a great deal through play and should be provided ample opportunities to engage in activities similar to those recommended for transitional kindergarteners.

Among the guidance and instructional suggestions for the grade are a discussion of the importance of thinking aloud while reading aloud to children (pp. 202–203), ways to support children's acquisition of academic language (pp. 205–206), suggestions for advancing writing development (pp. 207–208), the value of print-rich environments (p. 213), examples of phonological awareness (pp. 214–215), and the importance of attention to oral vocabulary when teaching beginning decoding—important for all students and crucial for ELs (pp. 216–217).

Grade One

Remarkable advances in literacy, language, and content knowledge occur during this grade. Children continue to learn skills that enable them to read and write with increasing independence. Special attention is given to ensuring that they are phonemically aware, know letter-sound and common spelling-sound correspondences, can accurately decode (sound out) regularly spelled one- and two-syllable printed words, and develop automaticity with the alphabetic system through ample practice of new learning in meaningful contexts. In addition to using their growing knowledge of the alphabetic system to read, children harness their understandings of the alphabetic code to share their own ideas and knowledge in writing. Initially, they spell words phonetically; as they progress, they employ common spelling patterns they are learning.

At the same time as foundational skills are being developed, meaning making is addressed; in fact, it undergirds all learning. Instruction in reading comprehension includes supporting children in identifying the central message or main topic of a text, understanding the purposes of various text features, and comparing and contrasting elements of texts. Children engage with a range of high-quality texts as listeners and readers. They participate in thoughtful discussions about texts and topics, learning how to build on the comments of others and to ask questions to clear up confusion or gather additional information. Ample time is devoted to enriching children's language and supporting their ability to express themselves effectively. Vocabulary development is given considerable attention. Concurrently, children have rich experiences in the content areas that expand their language and their knowledge of the world.

Among the guidance and instructional suggestions for the grade are examples of using context and word parts to gain meaning from unknown words (pp. 241–242); sample questions and sentence starters to promote children's responses to and building on the comments of others (p. 245); suggestions for children's presentations (pp. 245–246); ideas for decoding practice, including word building (pp. 249–251); and an example of teaching the blending of sounds (pp. 253–254).

Examples of Practice Provided in Snapshots (S) and Vignettes (V)

In transitional kindergarten

▶ Ms. Watson integrates foundational reading skills with mathematics as children learn to count syllables in spoken words. (S 3.1)

▶ Ms. Haddad guides children to retell a familiar story using books they constructed and props. (S 3.2)

▶ Mrs. Heaton integrates instruction in print concepts with art and science. (S 3.3)

▶ Ms. Campbell supports children's use of rich language as they jointly rewrite a story; during designated ELD, she guides ELs to use past tense verbs and expanded sentences. (V 3.1, 3.2).

In kindergarten

▶ Mr. Kravitz engages children in a literacy-, language-, and content-rich project on caring for their local environment. (S 3.4)

▶ Ms. Miller uses children's literature as a springboard for civic learning. (S 3.5)

▶ Mr. Hunt provides designated ELD that builds from children's observations of insects during science instruction. (S 3.6)

▶ Teachers in an alternative dual language program provide designated ELD through interactive read-aloud experiences. (S 3.7)

▶ Mr. Nguyen prompts meaning making, language development, and effective expression as he interactively reads aloud *Wolf* by Becky Bloom and Pascal Biet; his designated ELD lesson focuses on ELs' meaningful use of general academic vocabulary from the story. (V 3.3, 3.4)

In grade one

▶ Miss Zielonka guides children's understanding of the purpose of a table of contents in an informational text. (S 3.8)

▶ Mr. Rodriguez actively engages his students in learning science vocabulary crucial to their understanding concepts in a unit of study. (S 3.9)

▶ Mrs. Noguchi facilitates children's talk about math word problems during designated ELD. (S 3.10)

▶ Mr. Dupont supports ELs' use of expanded sentences and general academic and domain-specific vocabulary relevant to a social studies unit on American and international heroes. (S 3.11)

▶ Mrs. Fabian guides children's close reading of a passage about bees; during designated ELD, she demonstrates how to *unpack* complex sentences drawn from the informational texts. (V 3.5, 3.6)

Grades Two and Three

Grades two and three are exciting years as children become increasingly fluent with written language. They use their knowledge of the alphabetic code and of language in general to achieve their own goals as readers and writers. They engage with progressively more complex high-quality literary and informational text, expand their knowledge in the content areas, and continue to develop as effective communicators.

The grades two and three span is a pivotal time for children as they acquire more sophisticated comprehension, language, and decoding skills and develop the fluency necessary to propel them into more advanced reading, including independent reading of chapter books and grade-appropriate complex texts. Vocabulary development for meaning making, effective expression, and knowledge acquisition is a significant focus across the disciplines. Accuracy and automaticity in decoding, too, are high priorities, and children are provided ample opportunities to employ their skills as readers and writers in meaningful contexts. Children participate in content area investigations, conduct research, and engage in extended academic conversations with others daily.

Content and pedagogy in the grade span include the following:

- **Meaning Making** – Teachers facilitate literal and inferential comprehension, and they teach students to reread text for different purposes. Children learn to refer explicitly to the text as the basis for answers to questions about the text. They also learn how images contribute to meaning. Children determine and recount main ideas and supporting details of a text read aloud or information presented in diverse media and formats. They convey meaning in discussions and presentations.

- **Language Development** – Children continue to be exposed to rich language (through teacher modeling and read-aloud texts) and engage in purposeful use of language in meaningful, stimulating contexts. Systematic attention is given to vocabulary development. Children use glossaries and beginning dictionaries, both print and digital, to determine or clarify the meaning of words and phrases in all content areas, and they learn morphological units of words (e.g., prefixes). Children increase their awareness of language, describing how words and phrases supply rhythm and meaning in a story, poem, or song, and comparing formal and informal uses of English.

- **Effective Expression** – Children build on previous learning to write more detailed and cohesive texts for a variety of purposes across the disciplines. They learn to use feedback to revise and edit their work. They become more skilled in discussions. Teachers ensure topics are sufficiently compelling to spark discussion, prepare higher-order questions that prompt deep thinking, ask follow-up questions, and provide opportunities for children to lead discussions. Children plan and deliver presentations. They gain increasing command over oral and written language conventions.

- **Content Knowledge** – All students have full access to science, history/social studies, the arts, and all other content instruction, which is integrated with literacy and language. Students also engage in wide reading, including organized independent reading; interact with high-quality informational texts; and engage in research projects—all of which contribute to their knowledge.

- **Foundational Skills** – Foundational skills continue to be systematically taught during the grade span. Children learn to read multisyllabic words and words with complex spelling patterns. The number of high-frequency irregularly spelled words they can recognize effortlessly increases substantially. Fluency is a high priority, and children have many opportunities to engage in independent reading.

English learners engage in the same intellectually stimulating content through careful scaffolding and guidance provided by the CA ELD Standards. Concurrently, they are learning English as an additional language and receiving instruction that attends to their steady progress along the ELD continuum. Oral language development continues to be a significant emphasis during this grade span, and children have many opportunities to use language for different purposes in varied, meaningful contexts. Instruction capitalizes on the cultural and language resources each child brings to the classroom.

Grade Two

Children engage meaningfully with increasingly complex texts. They are read aloud to daily, and teachers model and discuss how to navigate challenging words, sentences, and passages to determine meaning. Children begin to write well organized, detailed texts of different genres, especially in response to texts and topics under investigation in different subject areas. They plan and deliver presentations.

Teachers give considerable attention to ensuring that children learn the remaining common spelling-sound correspondences and can accurately decode two-syllable words and words with common prefixes. They provide support and practice so children can decode nearly effortlessly. Children engage in wide and independent reading and have access to high-quality literary and informational text on a range of topics.

> **Among many figures included in chapter 4 are ones that**
> - describe research-based comprehension strategies;
> - provide examples of the rich language of children's literature;
> - identify trade books and other texts on grade-level topics;
> - describe stages of spelling development;
> - define and provide examples of Engish syllable types;
> - provide general guidance for teaching foundational skills to EL children;
> - provide examples of text-dependent and text-independent questions.

Among the guidance and instructional suggestions for the grade are a discussion of meaning making with complex text (pp. 290–293), strategies for supporting children's writing development (p. 322), formative assessment processes for writing (p. 300), tips for developing children's spelling knowledge (p. 325), and a description of a word-building activity in which children apply their phonics knowledge (pp. 328–329).

Grade Three

As readers and listeners, students learn to distinguish their own point of view from that of the author, narrator, or characters. They also distinguish shades of meaning and literal from nonliteral language, and they describe the logical connection between sentences and paragraphs in a text. They prepare for discussions, presentations, and writing, and they choose words and phrases for effect. Students begin to develop skill in keyboarding and cursive. Students learn the meaning

of most common prefixes and derivational suffixes, and they build skill in decoding multisyllabic words, including those with Latin suffixes.

Among the guidance and instructional suggestions for the grade are writing practices that improve reading comprehension (pp. 352–353), tips for children to give and receive constructive feedback on written work (p. 355), suggestions for ways children can prepare for discussions (pp. 358–359), and strategies for teaching children how to decode multisyllabic words (p. 364).

Examples of Practice Provided in Snapshots (S) and Vignettes (V)

In grade two

▸ Students engage in a hands-on activity to explore erosion and then take photographs of erosion in their local surroundings. They develop a digital presentation to share with peers in another class. (S 4.1)

▸ Ms. Li's students work in teams to write accordion books about pine cones after a "mystery bag" activity that prompted descriptive words, exploration of pine cones, and examination of supporting texts. (S 4.2)

▸ During designated ELD, Mr. Chen facilitates discussions by his ELs at the Bridging level of English language proficiency about content from a science unit on ecosystems. (S 4.3)

▸ Mr. Torres focuses on general academic language drawn from a social studies unit on civil rights heroes during designated ELD with ELs at the Emerging level of English language proficiency. (S 4.4)

▸ Mrs. Cooper works with a small group of ELs at the Expanding level of English language proficiency to help them ask and answer questions about problem solving using mathematical language. (S 4.5)

▸ As part of an author study, Mrs. Hernandez's students discuss questions that prompt the use of text evidence to support inference making; during designated ELD, students examine the author's use of verbs to convey how a character is feeling. (V 4.1, 4.2)

In grade three

▸ Students select and share with one another "powerful passages" from a work of literature and explain their choices. (S 4.6)

▸ Students collaborate to create morphing tableaux of important acts of American heroes. (S 4.7)

▸ Science, math, theatre, visual arts, and ELA are integrated in students' efforts to create a bird-nesting environment. (S 4.8)

▸ Ms. Barkley's students develop a classroom constitution at the beginning of the school year. (S 4.9)

▸ During designated ELD, Ms. Langer teaches a group of ELs at the Expanding level of English language proficiency about linking words and transitional phrases. (S 4.10)

▸ Mr. Franklin supports students in collaborative summarizing of informational text during integrated ELA and science instruction; during designated ELD, students who are ELs at the Expanding level of English language proficiency analyze complex sentences from the texts. (V 4.3, 4.4)

Grades Four and Five

Excellent instruction in the first years of schooling is imperative, but it does not guarantee success in the years ahead. Older students—those in grade four and above—must also be provided excellent instruction.

This grade span is a critically important time as students consolidate their skills and apply them across content areas, in different settings, and for different purposes. Students engage in voluminous independent reading and rich subject matter. Attention is given to keeping motivation high, especially through student choice and peer collaboration, as students encounter increasingly challenging texts and tasks.

Content and pedagogy in the grade span include the following:

- **Meaning Making** – Meaning making is the central focus of instruction. Students read exceptional literary and informational texts and share their understandings, insights, and responses with others. They draw evidence from texts to support analysis, reflection, and research; they identify the evidence a speaker or media source provides to support particular points. They engage deeply with content in all subject matter as readers, listeners, writers, researchers, and discussants—and through hands-on investigations.

- **Language Development** – Language development is an ongoing focus of instruction. Special attention is given in this span to learning and purposefully using general and domain-specific academic language. Students use context and morphology as clues to the meaning of words, and they consult a variety of reference materials to clarify the precise meaning of key words and phrases and to identify alternate word choices. They expand, combine, and reduce sentences for meaning, interest, and style. They use transitional words, phrases, and clauses to create cohesion.

- **Effective Expression** – Students produce multiple-paragraph texts in which the development and organization are appropriate to the task, purpose, and audience. They plan, revise, and edit their work. They become increasingly fluent in keyboarding. Students give well-organized, detailed presentations using multimedia. They learn about register and adapt their speech as appropriate for the context.

- **Content Knowledge** – All students have full access to content instruction, which is integrated with literacy and language. Students also engage in wide reading, including organized independent reading; interact with high-quality informational texts; and engage in research projects—all of which contribute to their knowledge.

- **Foundational Skills** – Students know and readily apply phonics and word analysis skills, including syllabication and morphological analysis, in decoding words. They read with sufficient fluency to support comprehension. Teachers provide instructional support as needed for individual learners, and they provide plentiful opportunities for students to engage in independent reading.

English learners participate in intellectually stimulating instruction as they are learning English as an additional language. Planned and just-in-time scaffolding ensure progress. The path ELs take as they develop academic English requires risk-taking, and students will likely make approximations with word choice, grammar, and oral discourse practices as they gain new understandings.

Steady advancement is best supported in a respectful setting that focuses on meaningful interactions relevant to content under study. Feedback should be strategically chosen, timely, and judicious.

Grade Four

Students in grade four experience the shift from primary to upper elementary school. They take on more complex texts across all subject matter. They determine themes in literary text and the main ideas presented in informational text. They attend to details and text structures and features. They interpret information presented in different forms, such as diagrams and animations. A significant milestone is that students write clear and coherent multi-paragraph texts. They also keyboard a minimum of one page in a single setting. Their writing incorporates detail, precise language, and linking words and phrases. Vocabulary instruction targets the use of Greek and Latin affixes and roots as clues to the meaning of a word. Importantly, students learn to differentiate between contexts that call for formal English and informal English.

Among many figures included in chapter 5 are ones that

▸ discuss research on motivation and engagement;

▸ define the components of the writing process;

▸ provide a brief guide on creating questions to prompt close, analytic reading of complex text;

▸ offer examples of Greek and Latin roots;

▸ describe discussant roles in literature circles;

▸ provide definitions and examples of grammar/usage terminology.

Among the guidance and instructional suggestions for the grade are suggestions for guiding students' efforts to comprehend, enjoy, and learn from complex text (p. 426), a discussion of the components of vocabulary instruction (pp. 427–428), and open sentence frames to facilitate students' use of sophisticated phrases and grammatical structures (p. 429).

Grade Five

Students approach text with greater purpose and critical stances. They voice their views in light of multiple perspectives and textual evidence. They begin to realize that they can interact with a text in ways that allow them to more deeply understand the text's meaning and also question its premises. Students use several sources when conducting research projects. Their language and knowledge continue to expand as they engage in voluminous reading and participate in rich content instruction. They learn about the varieties of English used in stories, dramas, or poems. They also become skilled at keyboarding, typing a minimum of two pages in a single setting, and use technology and media to learn and to share their ideas. Foundational skills are used effortlessly; reinforcement is provided as necessary to ensure fluency with print.

Among the guidance and instructional suggestions for the grade are suggestions for deeply engaging students with text (pp. 465–466), examples of support for ELs at different levels of English proficiency (pp. 481–482), and examples of language for cohesion (p. 497).

Examples of Practice Provided in Snapshots (S) and Vignettes (V)

In grade four

▸ Mr. Duarte involves students in a structured activity in which they mingle to review the concepts underlying domain-specific vocabulary from a California Gold Rush unit. (S 5.1)

▸ Mrs. Binder's students select important words from an informational text on volcanoes, build a histogram, discuss the words, and then write one-sentence summaries. (S 5.2)

▸ Mrs. Thomas provides designated ELD instruction that focuses on making inferences about characters based on their actions or feelings. She uses examples from a short story read by the class. (S 5.3)

▸ Mr. Jones works with EL students at the early Emerging level of proficiency during designated ELD instruction to examine verb use in discussions of geometric shapes. (S 5.4)

▸ Mrs. Patel's students examine the organization and language (e.g., grammatical structures and vocabulary) of several biographies and later jointly construct one about Dr. Martin Luther King, Jr.; during designated ELD instruction, students are grouped by proficiency level to meet with one of the team of teachers to learn and use new terms relevant to the biography unit. (V 5.1, 5.2)

In grade five

▸ Mrs. Louis-Dewar integrates the visual arts and ELA/literacy to teach sentence combining. (S 5.5)

▸ Mr. Hubert's students initiate a research and action project in response to a problem with mud in their classroom. (S 5.6)

▸ Ms. Johnson's students collaborate to create a silent film. (S 5.7)

▸ Ms. Brouhard's class engages in close reading of two drafts of the Preamble to the Constitution. (S 5.8)

▸ Ms. Avila conducts an integrated ELA/global art mini-lesson in which students discuss images of art from different regions of the world, especially those from which her students or their families immigrated. Designated ELD instruction supports ELs' use of new vocabulary from the lesson. (S 5.9)

▸ Mr. Rodriguez's students conduct research and write reports on ecosystems. As part of the instructional sequence, he engages students in text reconstruction of a short section from a relevant informational text; during designated ELD instruction, he teaches his ELs how to identify words and phrases that create cohesion in the science texts they have read on ecosystems. (V 5.3, 5.4)

Middle School

Young adolescents' quest for autonomy, relevance, meaning, and competence begins in earnest during these years, and motivation and engagement are critical factors in students' school success. Importantly, as middle school students explore the various layers of their identities, the adults around them exude acceptance, understanding, and validation of who they are as individuals and as members of various cultural, linguistic, religious, and other groups.

The CA CCSS for ELA/Literacy at this grade span represent a big leap for students as they move from the elementary grades to the middle grades, and the expanding cognitive abilities of these young adolescents position them to make big strides in ELA/literacy. Moving beyond details and examples, students now are expected to cite textual evidence to support their analysis of what the text states explicitly and what they infer from it. Argument is introduced at grade six, and students are expected to trace and evaluate arguments and claims in texts and write their own arguments, rather than opinions, supporting claims with clear reasons and relevant evidence. The CA ELD Standards also introduce argument at these grades, echoing the growing sophistication of the thinking expected at this level. New to grades six through eight are specific literacy standards in history/social studies, science, and technical subjects for the strands of reading and writing. Not only do students engage in careful analyses of texts in English language arts, they do so in history/social studies, science, mathematics, arts, world language, health, and physical education as well. In addition, students write to argue, explain, and inform in all areas of the curricula.

Content and pedagogy in the grade span include the following:

- **Meaning Making** – In this grade span, significantly more rigorous concepts of evidence, argumentation, and integration and analysis of multiple sources and perspectives emerge in meaning making.

- **Language Development** – All students continue to develop as learners of language throughout their academic careers, and indeed their lives. The development of academic English is critical for successful and equitable school participation in middle school and includes an intensive focus on vocabulary and grammatical understandings.

- **Effective Expression** – Students become increasingly effective at expressing themselves through different genres of writing and build on previous learning to write more complex and cohesive texts of different types for various purposes. They continue to develop and organize their writing in a way that is appropriate to the task, purpose, and audience. They increase their skill in discussing, presenting, and using language conventions successfully.

- **Content Knowledge** – Students engage in a full program of ELA and content instruction regardless of language proficiency or special needs. They study a range and variety of important works of literature and informational texts in all disciplines and through independent reading and research. They participate in an organized independent reading program that contributes to their knowledge.

- **Foundational Skills** – Ideally, students' knowledge of foundational skills is well established by the time they enter middle school, and they access and produce printed language efficiently. Teachers continue to support students' developing reading fluency to aid comprehension. Support for students who lag significantly behind in foundational reading skills is provided strategically and effectively to allow for accelerated progress and full participation in core instruction.

Students who are ELs engage in all of these academic activities at the same time they are learning English as an additional language, and some students may be simultaneously developing literacy and academic skills in languages other than English. The integration of ELD in ELA and all academic content courses necessitates collaboration among ELD and content area instructors. All teachers become teachers of the language needed to understand, engage with, and communicate about written texts, digital formats, and oral discourse in each discipline. As the CA ELD Standards intersect with and amplify the CA CCSS for ELA/Literacy, ELs at this grade span learn to explain ideas, phenomena, processes, and relationships based on close reading of texts in which they make inferences and draw conclusions. Critical for all students is the implementation of culturally responsive pedagogy and the development of positive and respectful relationships in all classrooms.

> **Among many figures included in chapter 6 are ones that**
>
> ▶ discuss research on motivation and engagement;
>
> ▶ define the components of the writing process;
>
> ▶ provide a brief guide on creating questions to prompt close, analytic reading of complex text;
>
> ▶ offer examples of Greek and Latin roots;
>
> ▶ describe discussant roles in literature circles;
>
> ▶ provide definitions and examples of grammar/usage terminology.

Grade Six

Grade six is often the first year of middle school for students and represents a major transition in students' lives. Just entering adolescence, these students eagerly encounter new areas of study and new ways to express their growing literacy understandings. This grade also represents a significant step in both sets of standards: argument replaces opinion in reading, speaking, and writing; separate literacy standards in the content areas make clear the literacy practices important in different disciplines; and thesis statements are expected in writing informative/ explanatory texts. All students engage in meaningful collaborations with peers, read and savor new and exciting literature, and deepen their knowledge of academic English. Students who are ELs receive rich instruction in all content areas and a comprehensive program of English language development.

In addition to the figures and snapshots, guidance and instructional suggestions for grade six include samples of text-dependent questions (pp. 551–552) and small group roles for discussions about nonfiction texts (pp. 559–561).

Grade Seven

Seventh graders may be in their first year of junior high school or in their second year of a sixth- through eighth-grade middle school program; in either case, they are expected to continue advancing their skills as they engage with ideas, concepts, and knowledge in literature and informational text in what they read in school and independently. They strengthen their reading and writing skills not just in the language arts, but across the content areas of history/social studies, science, and technical subjects. Students entering school as ELs, or who have been in U.S. schools since the elementary years but are still designated as ELs, need particular attention, as their English language and literacy abilities need to improve in an *accelerated time frame* for them to be prepared for the rigors of high school in two more years.

In addition to the figures and snapshots, guidance and instructional suggestions for grade seven include a five-word summary strategy (p. 583), reading comprehension strategies (p. 584), and sentence starters for discussions (p. 592).

Grade Eight

Generally, eighth graders are in their last year of junior high school or middle school and are preparing to meet the rigors of a high school program designed to help them meet the goals of ELA/literacy instruction needed for postsecondary education, careers, and civic life. In grade eight, the level of rigor and text complexity continues to increase from earlier grades as students also increase in their ability to generate meaningful analysis and demonstrate understanding. Students now analyze and present relationships and connections among ideas and information in reading, writing, and speaking. All students, and especially ELs, receive particular attention to help them transition successfully to high school.

In addition to the figures and snapshots, guidance and instructional suggestions for grade eight include procedures for identifying main ideas and developing a summary (pp. 618–619), strategies for building metalinguistic awareness of language and its conventions (pp. 619–620), and ways to vary purposes and time frames in a recursive writing process (p. 623).

Examples of Practice Provided in Snapshots (S) and Vignettes (V)

In grade six

▸ Ms. Chanthavong helps her students build language resources to summarize and analyze stories during designated ELD. (S 6.1)

▸ Mr. Powell supports his students to read complex texts and write arguments related to slavery in world history during designated ELD. (S 6.2)

▸ Ms. Smith teaches a unit in which students choose and defend a unit of data analysis in mathematics and integrated literacy. (S 6.3)

▸ Mr. Pletcher leads his students in a historical investigation, in which his students use primary and secondary sources, write responses, and participate in discussions. (S 6.4)

▸ Ms. Valenti engages her students in the close reading of a memoir, "The Making of a Scientist"; in designated ELD, Ms. Valenti guides her students to analyze the language of the text. (V 6.1, 6.2)

In grade seven

▸ Mr. Schoen engages students with a science text and demonstration of chemical reactions and guides them in making inferences. (S 6.5)

▸ During designated ELD, teachers and students examine the language resources used in science texts and tasks related to earthquakes. (S 6.6)

▸ Students at Bridges Middle School create and perform spoken word poetry. (S 6.7)

▸ During designated ELD, teachers guide students to construct and critique arguments in mathematics. (S. 6.8)

▸ Mrs. Massimo collaborates with an interdisciplinary team to teach the unit, "You Are What You Eat," and engages her students in close reading of informational text; during designated ELD, Ms. Quincy helps her students analyze text organization and persuasive language of the unit's texts. (V 6.3, 6.4)

In grade eight

▸ Ms. Okonjo leads her students to examine the vocabulary and syntax of a text as they consider issues of cyberbullying and civic learning. (S 6.9)

▸ Mrs. Wilson and Mr. Gato co-teach a lesson on Frederick Douglass and help their students analyze the language of the text during designated ELD. (S 6.10)

▸ Teachers at Fred Korematsu Middle School collaborate to teach a unit on the effects of human activity on the health of the earth in which they build students' skill in reading and writing arguments in science. (S 6.11)

▸ Mr. Franklin, Ms. Austin, and Mrs. García collaborate to teach a unit examining freedom of speech, including primary source documents; during designated ELD, Mrs. García supports her students to use scholarly discourse to debate issues. (V 6.5, 6.6)

High School

Navigating the highs and lows of adolescence, thoughtful and perceptive teachers help students expand their world views beyond the confines of the school and community.

The standards at this grade span represent increasingly sophisticated expectations for students. Students are prompted to think and operate at levels that result in the achievement of the College and Career Readiness Anchor Standards in Reading, Writing, Speaking and Listening, and Language by the end of grade twelve. Students' progress through the high school years sees many cognitive, physical, emotional, and social changes as these emerging adults contemplate their future and their place in the world around them. Adolescent brain development continues apace, and teen brains change and become more powerful every day.

Poised to exercise their language and literacy muscles, students engage with interesting inquiries, inspirational literature, and the deep questions of humanity. They turn their developing competencies to tasks that engage with real issues of the day (and yesterday) and are motivated by teachers, settings, and tasks that challenge their own and others' thinking and that honor their emerging stances and arguments. The depth of knowledge and level of thinking reflected in the standards are commensurate with the work that students will do in postsecondary education and careers.

Content and pedagogy in the grade span include the following:

- **Meaning Making** – Students engage in increasingly sophisticated levels of analysis and interpretation in their reading, listening, speaking, and writing. They are expected to analyze, evaluate, and address multiple authors, sources, motivations, representations, perspectives and points of view, themes and ideas, and interpretations as they read, write, speak, and listen.

- **Language Development** – Students come to understand and analyze how the structure of language and its organization in a variety of texts differ across academic disciplines, and they need to apply and adapt language forms and features to express their own ideas and construct arguments as appropriate to purpose, audience, and a range of formal and informal academic tasks.

- **Effective Expression** – Students become increasingly effective at expressing themselves through different genres of writing using specific rhetorical devices to support assertions. They synthesize multiple sources in their writing and synthesize comments, claims, and evidence on all sides of an issue in collaborative discussions. Students develop and deliver increasingly sophisticated presentations on complex and varied topics. They use words, phrases, clauses, and varied syntax to link major sections of text.

- **Content Knowledge** – Literacy is an essential tool for learning in every content area and preparing for postsecondary futures. Students wield appropriate literacy tools in all the disciplines they study. They engage with literary and informational text participating in cross-disciplinary explorations and research projects. Wide reading supports their acquisition of knowledge in ELA and other disciplines. Participation in an organized independent reading program contributes to their knowledge.

- **Foundational Skills** – Ideally, students' knowledge of foundational skills is well established by the time they enter high school, and they access and produce printed language efficiently. However, students who for a variety of reasons have not developed proficiency in the foundational reading skills at this point need intensive instruction in these skills, so they can access grade-level content as soon as possible.

English learners continue to advance their language and thinking at these grade levels in preparation for college and careers. As they progress along the ELD continuum, they are expected to understand and use appropriate registers to express and defend nuanced opinions, consider context in adapting language choices, and address complex questions and show thoughtful consideration of ideas and arguments. They also are asked to analyze the effects of language choices made by writers and speakers and make connections and distinctions between ideas and texts based on evidence as they persuade others. As is the case for ELs at all ages, educators need to monitor progress carefully to ensure that teaching and learning experiences attend to the particular learning needs of individuals. Understanding students' varied schooling experiences and English and primary language proficiencies helps teachers and schools ensure that each EL adolescent receives the academic challenge and support he or she needs to pursue his or her college and career aspirations.

Among many figures included in chapter 7 are ones that

▸ outline characteristics of good readers;

▸ note features of writing needed for success in postsecondary education;

▸ highlight elements of dialogic instruction;

▸ define disciplinary literacy in science, history, mathematics, and language arts;

▸ provide samples of paired literary and informational texts;

▸ provide a model for rhetorical analysis of reading and writing.

Grades Nine and Ten

The first year of high school is an exciting but anxious time for students. In the midst of one of the biggest transitions students make in their academic careers, they enter a new world of high school ELA and literacy in which they encounter new ideas, universal themes, and new demands in reading, writing, speaking, and listening. Students exercise new-found independence as they grapple with more complex ideas and an increased volume of reading and writing.

Students at grades nine and ten are called on to deploy their language and literacy skills to understand, interpret, and create text in ELA and all other subjects. Text complexity increases at these grades as students read Shakespeare and other works of world literature for the first time as well as textbooks and other sources in history/social studies, biology, health, geometry, and more. The standards expect students to question more and consider the impact of authors' choices of language and text structure.

For some students, this may be the first time they consider that a content area text may not represent indisputable truth or that literary text can be interrogated for its choices in presentation and ideas. The concept of the author as an imperfect individual is novel for many.

In addition to the figures and snapshots, guidance and instructional suggestions for grades nine and ten include strategies for classroom discussion (pp. 724–725) and Socratic Seminars (p. 731).

Grades Eleven and Twelve

The final two years of high school are full of plans—plans for college, for careers, and for for their future lives. Students are now at their most independent and are poised to make yet another momentous transition. In ELA and other content areas, students are increasingly sophisticated in their thinking and performances displaying a critical and thoughtful stance toward their coursework and the problems of the day. Their reasoning and debating skills never better, they welcome the opportunity to engage in meaningful discussions and debates. Expectations for the volume, pace, and depth of reading and writing increase to new levels.

Students at these grades read Shakespeare, seminal documents of U.S. history, and works of American literature as well as textbooks and other sources in government, civics, chemistry, precalculus, and more. Students are expected to determine where the text leaves matters uncertain, identify inconsistencies, and analyze how complex ideas interact and develop. Students also evaluate the effectiveness of structures the author uses and identify rhetoric that is particularly effective. The formal study of syntax is introduced and students are expected to vary its use in their writing. Students write arguments and make presentations using precise and knowledgeable claims and counterclaims, supplying the most relevant evidence, and anticipating the audience's knowledge level, concerns, values, and possible biases.

In addition to the figures and snapshots, guidance and instructional suggestions for grades eleven and twelve include reading with the grain and reading against the grain (p. 769) and analyzing and understanding complex syntax (p. 772).

Examples of Practice Provided in Snapshots (S) and Vignettes (V)

In grades nine and ten

▶ At Nelson Mandela Academy, students engage in collaborative discussions and reflect on their own histories of using language in different contexts as they create linguistic autobiographies. (S 7.1)

▶ Mrs. Arrowsmith guides her history students to examine India's independence movement and discuss various open-ended questions using a Socratic Seminar. (S 7.2)

▶ Mrs. Herrera leverages the structure of a mock trial to help students construct arguments as they read William Shakespeare's *MacBeth*. (S 7.3)

▶ Ms. Shankle guides her science students to formulate questions when reading about force and motion to monitor their understanding. (S 7.4)

▶ Los Rios High School provides a robust academic curriculum and specialized instructional support for newcomer English learners. (S 7.5)

▶ Ms. Alemi, world literature teacher, and Ms. Cruz, world history teacher, collaboratively teach a unit examining diverse perspectives in world literature using *Things Fall Apart* by Chinua Achebe; during designated ELD, Mr. Branson collaborates with Ms. Cruz to help EL students analyze language patterns from their history texts such as abstraction, agency, and causal relationships. (V 7.1, 7.2)

In grades eleven and twelve

▶ Ms. Fontana, grade twelve environmental science teacher, supports her students to read science texts related to water quality. (S 7.6)

▶ Mrs. Ellis teaches students to paraphrase in order to craft a sophisticated, well-supported argument using text from *King Lear*. (S 7.7)

▶ Ms. Oliver cultivates classroom conversations about the novel *Invisible Man*. (S 7.8)

▶ Mr. Lee guides his students in developing a communications campaign addressing the question: Why should anyone care about voting today? (S 7.9)

▶ Ms. Durán and her colleagues collaboratively design a unit in which students debate challenging topics of race, religion, and income. (S 7.10)

▶ Mr. Toft designs a graphic organizer for students to use in exploring topics in international trade in an economics class. (S 7.11)

▶ Mr. Jackson guides his students in an investigation of the President's war-making powers during the Vietnam War using primary sources. (S 7.12)

▶ Ms. Robertson guides her students to explore a range of perspectives about the Civil Rights Movement using informational texts and the book, *Bury My Heart at Wounded Knee*; during designated ELD Mr. Martinez guides his students to unpack sentences and understand nominalization in the same texts. (V 7.3, 7.4)

Topic-Specific Guidance

In addition to grade-level guidance, the *ELA/ELD Framework* provides guidance on specialized topics in chapters 8 through 12. Rich in detail, the chapters support teachers, specialists, and administrators as they organize programs in English language arts, literacy across the content areas, and English language development. Brief summaries of each chapter are provided in this section.

Assessment

Assessment has two fundamental purposes: One is to provide information about student learning minute-by-minute, day-to-day, and week-to-week so that teachers continuously adapt instruction to meet students' specific needs and secure progress. This type of assessment is intended to assist learning and is often referred to as **formative assessment** or **assessment *for* learning**. A second purpose of assessment is to provide information on students' current levels of achievement after a period of learning has occurred. Such assessments—which may be classroom-based, districtwide, or statewide—serve a **summative** purpose and are sometimes referred to as **assessments *of* learning**.

Skilled use of assessment tools and processes is critical for ensuring students' achievement in ELA/literacy and ELD. Only when teachers and leaders have a range of accurate information about student learning are they in a position to make decisions that advance learning.

Chapter 8 (Assessment) includes numerous figures (e.g., types and uses of assessments, a rubric for scoring essays, a form for collaborative conversation observation notes), and snapshots of assessment in action (e.g., formative assessment with secondary EL newcomers, interim assessment in grade one, student involvement in assessment in grade four, and peer feedback in grade three). The chapter also includes guidance for progress monitoring for ELs.

Access and Equity

The *ELA/ELD Framework* was written with the rich diversity of California's population in mind and calls for public education that supports all learners toward achieving their highest potential. Schools ensure the following:

- Educators plan instruction appropriate for the **range of learners** in their classrooms (i.e., Universal Design for Learning).
- Schools and districts have a **clear system** in place for supporting students (i.e., Multi-Tiered System of Supports).
- Instruction is **culturally and linguistically responsive**.

Chapter 9 (Access and Equity) includes discussions of the unique needs of several populations of learners (e.g., English learners; Standard English learners [speakers of African American English and Chicana/Chicano English]; students who are deaf and bilingual in ASL and printed English;

students living in poverty; students who are migrants; students who are lesbian, gay, bisexual, or transgender; students with disabilities; advanced learners). These populations are heterogeneous and not mutually exclusive, and although general guidance is provided, each student should be recognized as an individual.

Also included in the chapter are numerous figures (e.g., poverty and classroom engagement issues and actions, types of accommodations for students with disabilities, UDL principles and guidelines, new ways of talking about language, strategies for supporting learners' engagement with complex text) and snapshots of practice (e.g., differentiated instruction in a co-taught language arts class in grade nine, direct instruction of metaphors with grade-four students who have a learning disability and those experiencing difficulty in ELA).

Learning in the 21st Century

Skills for living and learning in the 21st century are inextricably linked with achievement of the ELA/literacy and ELD standards. Among these skills are the four "C's" (critical thinking, creative thinking, communication, and collaboration), social and cross-cultural skills and global competence, and technology skills. Several examples of the relationship between these skills and the standards are provided in the following figure. (See p. 962 in the framework for the complete figure.)

All students should have access to curricula, instruction, and learning environments that develop their 21st century skills. Chapter 10 includes numerous figures and snapshots of practice (e.g., creating an online Cold War museum exhibit in grade eleven, integrating technology into an extended science writing project in grade two, producing electronic book trailers in grade six).

Students develop	when they...
Critical thinking	▸ examine text closely to interpret information, draw conclusions, and evaluate an author's decisions about content and form ▸ identify an author's perspectives, biases, and use of rhetoric
Creative thinking	▸ develop dramatic, poetic, media, and visual responses to text ▸ create presentations to share understandings of text
Communication and collaboration skills	▸ interact in meaningful ways with peers of diverse backgrounds and discuss different and similar perspectives on issues ▸ plan and organize collaborative presentations
Social and cross-cultural skills and global competence	▸ engage with literature that presents a range of world perspectives and experiences ▸ capitalize on proficiency in languages other than English to communicate with global peers
Technology skills	▸ engage with digital and multimedia text ▸ use a variety of technologies to share information from or responses to texts or to learn more about a topic or author

Implementing High-Quality ELA/Literacy and ELD Instruction: Professional Learning, Leadership, and Program Supports

Successful implementation of the *ELA/ELD Framework* occurs within a collaborative and learning culture. It relies on commitment to continuous improvement that begins with an assessment of existing resources, systems, and professional knowledge and skill. Chapter 11 addresses three essential implementation components:

- **Professional learning** is the vehicle for all school staff—teachers, administrators, specialists, counselors, teacher librarians, and others—to learn to effectively implement the curricular and instructional practices proposed in this framework. Five research-based features should be incorporated in professional learning designs: content focus, active learning, coherence, duration, and collective participation. Ultimately, effective professional learning should mirror effective classroom instruction.

- **Leadership** in a collaborative and learning culture is distributed and shared; it is not limited to principals or other administrators and, in fact, promotes teacher leadership as a powerful means of establishing a healthy and collaborative school culture. Responsibility for student success is held in common and transcends grade-level and departmental boundaries.

- **Program supports** include specialist services, libraries and media centers, and extended learning opportunities for students. They also include communication and collaboration with parents and families and partnerships with community groups and other institutions.

Through collaborative professional structures, teachers and other educators focus on professional improvement to achieve the student improvement envisioned in the *ELA/ELD Framework*.

Figures in chapter 11 present standards and list critical content for professional learning, display unique needs of ELs to consider in program improvement, examine types and uses of assessment, offer a sample plan to monitor ELD progress, present models of co-teaching, and depict principles and guidance for parent involvement.

Instructional Materials to Support the CA CCSS for ELA/Literacy and CA ELD Standards

Instructional materials should reflect the vision set forth in the *ELA/ELD Framework* and promote students' progress through the grades. The criteria listed in chapter 12 of the framework describe crucial components of effective kindergarten through grade eight instructional programs that are aligned to the CA CCSS for ELA/Literacy, the CA ELD Standards, and the *ELA/ELD Framework*. Five programs are described in the chapter: ELA, ELA/ELD, biliteracy/ELD, intervention, and specialized designated ELD. Guidance is also provided on the adoption of instructional materials for students in grades nine through twelve. Districts have responsibility to adopt materials that best meet the needs of their students and to conduct an evaluation of instructional materials in accordance with California Education Code. For example, review committees must include a majority of classroom teachers from the content area or grade level, and involvement of parents and other members of the community must be promoted.

Conclusion

California is a vibrant and dynamic state of extraordinary global influence and is unsurpassed in its cultural and linguistic resources. California's schools are charged with preparing its children and youth for the incredible opportunities that await them. The adoption of the CA CCSS in ELA/Literacy and the CA ELD Standards and the development of the *ELA/ELD Framework* represent California's commitment to ensure that all its students receive an education that enables them to take advantage of possibilities, pursue their dreams, and contribute to the wellbeing of California and the world. The most promising futures await our students—and our society—when we ensure that all individuals acquire strong literacy and language skills in every discipline.